West Midlands ~~Travel~~
The First T~~en Years~~

In colour imagery by

Venture *publications*

Front Cover: The 40 Alexander RH bodied Scania N113DRBs would be the only new step-entrance double-deckers delivered to West Midlands Travel following the cessation of Metrobus production by MCW. They were allocated to Birmingham Central garage, principally for service 50 but could wander at times. In this view from April 1991, 3221 (H221LOM) had been deployed to service 900 from Birmingham to Coventry in place of the usual Timesaver vehicle. Within weeks, the beauty referred to on the vehicle's side advertisement would become inaccessible as Yugoslavia descended into civil war.

Frontispiece: After an overnight snowfall on 3 March 1995, roads on the approach to Dudley bus station had been cleared but the pavements still have a significant covering. MCW Metrobus Mark 2 2905 (C905FON), carrying WMBuses Hockley fleetnames, had arrived on service 120 and was awaiting its time to head for the departure bays. Unusually for a West Midlands Travel vehicle, it carried advertising either side of the destination screen in London Transport style. In this case, it is self-promoting for the on-bus advertising broker Outdoor Media. The previous appearance of such adverts on West Midlands Travel vehicles appears to date back to 1990 and a campaign for the book 'Daddy' on MCW Metrobuses at Birmingham Central garage.

© 2024 David Cole & MDS Book Sales T/A Venture Publications
ISBN 9781898432791

All rights reserved. Except for normal review purposes no part of this book may be reproduced or utilised in any form by any means, electrical or mechanical, including photocopying, recording or by an information storage and retrieval system, without the prior written consent of MDS Book Sales, Glossop, Derbyshire, SK13 8EH.
Design by ATGraphics, Peterborough

Introduction

Deregulation Day, 26 October 1986, brought wide-ranging changes to the bus industry across Great Britain, excluding London. Bus operation now had to be a commercial enterprise and local authorities were required to secure contracts with operators to provide any service that was considered socially necessary. The result was the biggest overnight upheaval in bus operations ever experienced. As a multitude of new and unfamiliar operators together with revised services from established operators took to the road, passengers found the changes challenging although at times they would benefit from lower fares, usually just for a short term. Deregulation did bring other benefits, at a stroke the ever-increasing rate of block grant paid to support services run by large nationalised or municipally owned operations ceased. The bus industry also became renowned for the entrepreneurial flair brought by new entrants and unshackled managers as the various publicly owned operations passed in to the private sector.

In the West Midlands' WMPTE's directly operational activities were transferred to West Midlands Travel, a company wholly owned at arms-length by the West Midlands' local authorities. This would be sold to its employees in 1991 (ESOP) before joining National Express in 1995 in lieu of taking its own route to a stock market flotation.

▲ West Midlands Travel recognised its heritage from pre-WMPTE days with the painting of a vehicle from each garage in the colours of the municipal undertaking that formerly operated in that locality. Several of the MCW Metrobus Mark 2 and Mark 2A vehicles involved gathered in the car park adjacent to the Aston Villa football ground on 14 July 1996. Only the former Walsall colours were not represented due to that vehicle being unserviceable on the day.

Author's note

Following the positive response to my first volume, WMPTE – The County Years, this second volume looks at the first ten years from Deregulation and covers three distinct phases: the arms-length years (1986-91), the ESOP years (1991-95) and the initial National Express years (1995 to the launch of the Travel West Midlands rebrand in October 1996). It concentrates on operations in the greater West Midlands with reference to the companies that West Midlands Travel acquired nationwide only included where vehicle movements took place in either direction. It is not intended to be a definitive history of West Midlands Travel, more a celebration of some of the vehicles that the company operated.

All images are my own with the exception of a few from my late friend John Whitmore (marked JW) to fill important gaps in the story. Caption information has been gathered from a wide variety of printed and online sources together with feedback from some of those involved in the business during the years covered to whom many thanks are extended.

David Cole
Bromsgrove
July 2024

PART 1 An 'Arms-Length' company
1.1 Vehicles transferred from WMPTE

The majority of West Midlands Travel's initial fleet was made up of Daimler Fleetlines, MCW Metrobuses and Leyland Nationals transferred from WMPTE. Service revisions and the new vehicles for 'Timesaver' and 'Mini Buzz' operations had enabled some rationalisation measures to take place. Out were the last of the Bristol VRTs, the last former Midland Red Leyland Nationals (for a few years at least!) and the last vehicles transferred from Coventry City Transport although many of the final batch of East Lancs bodied Leyland Fleetlines that the latter ordered and were delivered directly to WMPTE would enjoy a long service life with West Midlands Travel. Variety in the fleet was maintained by the batch of 50 Volvo Ailsas, the evaluation vehicles from 1985 and the two Duple Dominant Bus bodied Dennis Lancets used on special services in Coventry. Central Coachways operations including its early minibus applications also transferred to the new company.

◄ Although all West Midland Travel's original MCW Metrobuses appeared outwardly similar when the new branding was applied, there was a minority with significant differences under the skin. 22 examples had been bought by WMPTE with Rolls-Royce Eagle engines, two of which were pre-series vehicles. 7006/7 (BOM6/7V) entered service at a similar time to the first production examples but had been built around the time the PTE received its first pre-series vehicles in 1978 with interiors of that era and were intended to be test beds for a new locally produced gearbox. This failed to progress and a standard driveline with the Rolls-Royce engine replacing the usual Gardner model was installed. The Rolls-Royce engined examples were always associated with Acocks Green garage and 7006 was seen in May 1988, descending Carrs Lane in Birmingham city centre before the traffic flow was reversed in what remains a major bus artery in 2024.

▶ MCW bodied Leyland Fleetline 6585 (NOC585R), ascending Birmingham's Bull Ring in May 1988, showed the standard application of the West Midlands Travel brand to this vehicle type. Running apparently empty and out of service, the blind settings of the Yardley Wood based vehicle suggest a recent use on the revised Solihull area services introduced alongside the minibus network at deregulation. All the background buildings and greenery have since been swept away by redevelopment.

▲ Over two years after deregulation, Leyland National 1512 (TOE512N) still displayed the most basic of West Midlands Travel vinyl applications when imaged in West Bromwich's WMPTE era bus station during March 1989.

▶ The evaluation batches of Leyland Lynx and Alexander P type bodied Volvo Citybus had been repainted in an unbranded Metrobus style colour scheme shortly before deregulation and simply gained West Midlands Travel fleetnames on their blue panels. Transferred to Lea Hall garage by April 1989, Leyland Lynx 1066 (C66HOM) was seen in the approach road to Solihull railway station working the long 71 service which linked Solihull with Sutton Coldfield through Birmingham's eastern suburbs. The equivalent service in 2024 is split in Chelmsley Wood, the southern section to Solihull adopting the number 72.

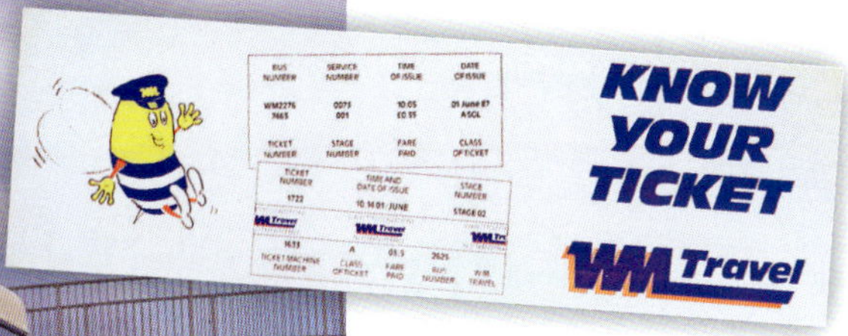

◀ With over 500 examples, the MCW Metrobus Mark 2 was the most common vehicle type in the initial West Midlands Travel fleet. 2737 (A737WVP) was a Harts Hill based vehicle and showed the typical application of its new operator's logos on its previous WMPTE colour scheme when departing Dudley on service 245 to Stourbridge on 21 March 1987.

▶ The ten short wheelbase Carlyle converted Ford Transits operated by Central Coachways on behalf of WMPTE passed to West Midlands Travel, gaining the Mini Buzz branding and fleetnumbers in the 5xx minibus range. In October 1987, 561 (B61AOP) was seen turning at the end of the Sutton New Road dual carriageway in Erdington prior to a local journey to Pype Hayes showing no service number.

▶ Other than the application of West Midlands Travel fleetnames and legal lettering, little changed with the vehicles used on Coventry's Easy Rider services through deregulation. In a scene reminiscent of the one in 'WMPTE The County Years' where they were incorrectly described as Dennis Javelins, Duple Dominant Bus bodied Dennis Lancet 1054 (B54AOC) stood in front of similar 1053 (B53AOC) in Coventry's Pool Meadow bus station late in 1987. JW

▶ The only vehicles associated with the former Coventry Corporation Transport to transfer to West Midland Travel were the forty East Lancashire bodied Leyland or Daimler FE30 Fleetlines which were ordered by Coventry but delivered to WMPTE in 1977. Apart from an early intermezzo at Acocks Green garage, all operated in Coventry for most of their lives. Unusually, on 4 February 1990, 6759 (SDA759S) was working from Quinton garage and was seen in Corporation Street, Birmingham departing on service 3 to Woodgate Valley North.

6

1.2 New vehicles for deregulation initiatives

In addition to registering a significant core of existing commercial services across the West Midlands boroughs, West Midlands Travel invested in two fleets of new vehicles to service commercial initiatives from Deregulation Day. 50 high specification MCW Metrobus Mark 2s for longer distance limited stop services across the region under the Timesaver brand and over 150 minibuses from five manufacturers, (Freight Rover, Ford, Iveco, Dodge and MCW) for local networks in Solihull, Sutton Coldfield and Cradley Heath. Not all of these were in service concurrently as MCW Metrorider deliveries replaced the interim Freight Rover Sherpas.

▶ Some, at least, of the 36 Carlyle bodied Freight Rover Sherpas arrived in advance of deregulation hence 517 (D517NDA) had yet to lose its WMPTE legal lettering when seen in Erdington in the Autumn of 1986 although carrying full West Midlands Travel Mini Buzz branding. All were replaced by MCW Metroriders within a year and 517 was one of 30 that were subsequently operated by Yorkshire Rider. JW

▼ 18 Reeve-Burgess (Reebur) bodied Dodge S56 minibuses were chosen for the minibus network based on the new interchange at Cradley Heath railway station. Alongside the DODGE lettering, 578 (D578NDA) also carried a badge for the manufacturers parent company, Renault, when seen leaving the interchange on 21 March 1987 bound for nearby Netherton.

7

▶ Once home of the first local dial-a-ride minibus network, minibuses returned to the Solihull area on a range of post deregulation lettered services. Arriving at Solihull station on 11 April 1987 working service A from Acocks Green via Olton, was 593 (D593NDA), one of 14 Iveco 49-10 TurboDailys bodied by Robin Hood Coachbuilders that provided the network's initial fleet. 594 from the same batch was displayed on the Iveco stand at the 1986 Motor Show prior to entering service.

▶ The initial West Midlands Travel fleet included ten short wheelbase Ford Transits that had been new in 1985 and operated initially by Central Coachways as M1-M10. These would later take the numbers 555-564 in the main fleet and be augmented by three long wheelbase examples, 552-554, again with Carlyle bodywork. One of the latter, 553 (D553NOE) was seen loading in Erdington for the local service to Pype Hayes on 25 August 1988, no provision has been made for a service number to be shown.

◀ The 50 MCW Mark 2 Metrobuses for the new Timesaver limited stop bus network were specified with coach seats and carpeted floors, reducing their passenger capacity by seven from the standard 73 of all previous Metrobuses except for the first prototype. They had four speed gearboxes and were initially easily distinguishable externally by their colour scheme that had been developed using one of the silver base Metrobuses then used on the Tracline 65 guided bus service. One vehicle, 2938 (D938NDA), was fitted with a Cummins engine instead of the usual Gardner unit and undertook some demonstration work with it, retaining it for life. 2936 (D936NDA) was additionally distinguished by carrying the name of Wolverhampton based athlete and sports ambassador, Tessa Sanderson, the first black woman to win Olympic gold for GB. It would be around 20 years before the naming of buses operated by West Midlands Travel's successors became standard practice. On 14 July 1989, 2936 was seen heading through Birmingham's Bull Ring bound for Coventry on the limited stop 900 service which at that time had a western terminus at Hasbury outside Halesowen.

MCW launched the Metrorider mini/midibus at the 1986 Motor Show at the NEC, an event overshadowed by the imminence of deregulation. Seen on 14 October 1986, one prototype, later registered D483NOX, was displayed in West Midlands Travel colours but would not be one of the 85 production vehicles that the company would acquire in 1987 and 1988. The West Midlands Travel examples were all short wheelbase models and were used initially to displace the Freight Rover Sherpas on the Sutton Coldfield Network and provided additional capacity for the Solihull Network. In October 1987, 624 (D624NOE), was working the 620 service in Erdington which required a U-turn on Sutton New Road's dual carriageway.

1.3 The colour scheme evolves

▶ Metrobus style livery with blue window surrounds had been applied to the 1985 evaluation vehicles when repainted in WMPTE days and would subsequently feature on Leyland Nationals and those Volvo Ailsas that received a repaint before all 50 were sold to London Transport in 1987. One of those so painted, 4778 (JOV778P), whistled towards Spaghetti Junction on a 104 service to Sutton Coldfield on 11 March 1987 showing evidence of damage to the rear offside corner.

Many of the dual-purpose seated Leyland Nationals received the silver Timesaver livery for limited stop services but 1829 (OOX829R) was turned out in blue and cream applied in Metrobus style with just a simple WM logo on the front. In Spring 1989, it was working the 226 between Dudley and Bilston, imaged here on Dudley's Castle Hill with the repurposed cinema in the background. In 2023, Castle Hill gained a reserved tram track for the Midland Metro extension to Brierley Hill.

10

◀ Having established the silver base colour on the Tracline and Timesaver vehicles, it was not long before a similar scheme was developed for the rest of the fleet although this would feature various shades of grey as well as silver as vehicles were repainted, grey proving to be more durable. One of the first grey repaints was MCW Metrobus Mark 2 2667 (ROX667Y), which had previously carried a series of advertising liveries. With banners for summer attractions above, it was seen heading up Corporation Street in Birmingham before the application of company branding.

◀ MCW Metrobus 2419 (LOA419X) received a silver base to its new colour scheme and looked very smart waiting on the approach road to Solihull station prior to departing as a service 6 to Birmingham city centre on 14 April 1989.

◀ A much lighter shade of grey had been applied to MCW Metrobus Mark 2 2740 (A740WVP) seen in ex-works condition departing Wolverhampton bus station on 3 May 1989. New destination blinds had yet to be installed so prospective passengers will hopefully know where the 513 service is headed for. Wolverhampton bus station has subsequently been comprehensively redeveloped.

On a snowy 8 February 1991, Leyland National 1837 (TVP837S) battled its way along Birmingham's Lister Street bound for the city centre on service 14 from Tile Cross. It carries the single-deck version of the grey colour scheme. In 2024, the 14 still serves Tile Cross but has been diverted via Duddeston on its way to the city centre and the 66 now runs along Lister Street, on the edge of Aston University's campus.

▲ Having gained Metrobus style livery in WMPTE days, the 1985 evaluation single-deckers were again refinished in the grey scheme. For the Leyland Lynx, the 'minimum blue' version used on the later production vehicles was applied. In the case of 1064 (C64HOM), loss of the lower trim panel at the rear has further reduced the blue area. On 10 March 1990, it was in Leamington on a private hire for the Merseyside Bus Club.

▲ The Volvo Citybuses with Alexander P type bodywork gained the standard blue and silver-grey colour scheme as displayed by 1060 (C60HOM) in Birmingham's Colmore Row on 8 September 1990, it was working the 79 service back to its Wolverhampton base. Normally double-decker operated, the 79 was an early WMPTE innovation linking together former Birmingham, West Bromwich and Wolverhampton municipal services, in 2024 it heads no further east than West Bromwich.

▲ An assortment of Daimler/Leyland Fleetlines gained the blue and silver scheme including 6688 (WDA688T), one of the final Park Royal bodied Leyland Fleetlines delivered to WMPTE. Seen working service 46 to Pheasey from Birmingham's New Street on 3 April 1990, a poorly applied new in-house advert reveals that the previous advert had not been removed when it was repainted.

▶ The small batch of 10.6m Leyland National 2s delivered to WMPTE in 1980 spent much of their operating career in all-over-advertising schemes so 7048 (DOC48V) presented an unusual sight freshly repainted in West Midland Travel's grey scheme although still at work on the Centrebus service. On 12 April 1990, it contrasted with spring foliage in Birmingham's Bull Ring, a location that would place it in the basement of Selfridges department store in 2024.

◀ An odd one out in West Midland Travel's highly standardised MCW Metrobus Mark 2 fleet was 2791 (B791AOC) which was equipped with an advanced (for its era) electronic destination display that allowed the service number and two lines of destination to be displayed. On 28 May 1991, it had arrived in Dudley bus station on service 311 from Walsall. The WMPTE era bus station closed in January 2024 to enable a West Midlands Metro halt to be installed where 2791 is standing.

▶ Timesaver evolves (top to bottom): At the bus rally held at Kidderminster Severn Valley Railway station on 8 October 1989, dual-purpose MCW Metrobus Mark 2 2931 (D931NDA) was entered by staff from Walsall garage carrying a revised Timesaver colour scheme featuring the bright grey base colour then being used on some standard repaints. A similar scheme but retaining a silver base was seen on 2937 (D937NDA) loading for Hednesford in Birmingham's Lower Bull Street in August 1990. A blue base colour, similar to that of Central Coachways then featured on a number of repaints with variations in lettering style. Early in 1990, 2956 (D956NDA) was in Edgbaston Street, Birmingham carrying a blue scheme relieved only by the Timesaver branding while 2914 (D914NDA) had just left the same stop heading for Coventry in early 1991 and carrying the blue scheme with gold lettering that was to feature on several Timesaver vehicles.

▶ Some minibuses were repainted a relatively short time after entering service including Reeve-Burgess (Reebur) bodied Dodge S56 minibus 572 (D572NDA) seen leaving Merry Hill shopping centre bus station on 25 November 1989. An RNLI lifeboat on a promotional tour is sharing space in the bus station with vehicles from the Merry Hill Minibuses fleet which would be a future West Midlands Travel acquisition.

▲ The standard application of the initial blue and grey scheme to the Leyland National mark 1 is demonstrated by 1525 (TOE525N) as it departed Dudley's WMPTE era bus station on 31 August 1993, The doors of the now 18 year old bus are open to aid visibility at the oblique junction on this exit from the bus station.

Before all the fleet had gained the blue and silver/grey scheme, a revised application with blue upperworks and a red stripe at waist level was introduced. The evolution of the scheme is clearly seen in this view of MCW Metrobus Mark 2s 2446 (NOA446X) and 2708 (A708UOE) as they departed in the West Bromwich direction from Walsall's Bradford Place on 7 September 1991. Aside from the evolved application of blue and red, the difference in silver and grey background colours is strongly highlighted and each bus has a different style of MCW badging.

▶ The MCW and Park Royal bodied Leyland Fleetlines looked very smart when repainted in the 'red stripe' scheme, enhanced on Coventry based MCW bodied 6922 (WDA922T) by the application of grey paint to the wheels. On 18 January 1992, it was parked in the layover area of Coventry's then Pool Meadow bus station prior to a trip on service 3 to Binley on the city's eastern outskirts. The bus station has subsequently been redeveloped and the passenger concourse now covers this layover area.

▶ In the 'red stripe' colour scheme with a grey background and blue wheels, MCW bodied Leyland Fleetline 6937 (WDA937T) and a tree in full spring blossom brightened up a dull and damp Bearwood bus station on 26 April 1990. It had arrived in Bearwood on service 82 from Birmingham city centre along the city's Dudley Road, known to bus crews as 'the track' since Midland Red and Birmingham City Transport buses replaced its trams in 1939.

▶ A number of MCW Metroriders received the 'red stripe' colour scheme including 633 (D633NOE) seen in West Bromwich's WMPTE era bus station on 1 September 1993 sporting mismatched wheel colours.

20

◀ In the 'red stripe' scheme on a silver base with what appear to be black wheels, East Lancs bodied Leyland Fleetline FE30 6746 (SDA746S) was seen loading in Broadgate, Coventry on 18 April 1992. Ordered by Coventry City Transport but delivered to WMPTE with many of the latter's standard fittings, this batch of Leyland Fleetlines although non-standard would lead full service lives with West Midlands Travel. It carries advertising celebrating the then recent buy out of the company through an Employee Share Option Plan (ESOP).

◀ When seen turning into West Bromwich's WMPTE era bus station on 4 September 1993, MCW bodied Daimler Fleetline 6881 (TVP881S) carried a long-lasting transitional colour scheme with blue upperworks and a thin low level red stripe on its lower blue panels. All of the infrastructure in the image has subsequently been swept away for the development of West Bromwich's Arts Centre (now a school in 2024) and the New Square shopping complex.

◀ WMPTE's first production MCW Metrobus numerically had migrated to Walsall depot and gained the 'red stripe' scheme on a silver base by 1994. On 11 April 1994, 2001 (BOK1V) was in Cannock bus station en route from Walsall to Hednesford. West Midlands Travel operated a significant network of services in the Cannock area before withdrawing from most operations outwith of the former West Midlands County.

1.4 (Mainly) new vehicles for the arm's length company

The deregulation era was a challenging time for the UK's bus manufacturers as the uncertainty created caused new full size vehicle orders to plummet. Several diversified into other activities including servicing the short-term minibus boom, others consolidated and would eventually close down or be acquired by other parties. The arms-length West Midlands Travel business was one of the first to offer a beacon of hope to the industry with an order for 150 new double-deckers for delivery in 1987-8. Not surprisingly, the order went to MCW for an improved Metrobus known as the Mark 2A. With the cessation of MCW production announced before all 150 were completed, delivery of the last few stretched into 1990 and only 149 would enter service with West Midlands Travel. The 'missing' vehicle 3107 (G107FJW) was sold by MCW as a sample vehicle with the rights to the Metrobus design to Optare Ltd and used in connection with the development of the latter's Spectre model. It subsequently passed to Capital Citybus, eventually joining First Group and being one of 100 buses donated to Asian states under the Asia Bus Response initiative following the 2003 Boxing Day Tsunami. Here it was united with other West Midlands Travel Metrobuses that had been donated directly.

Single-deck investment followed quickly, the Leyland Lynx being chosen after experience of the 1985 evaluation vehicles. The order was for 250 vehicles with delivery from 1988 to 1990, 15 of them arrived with dual-purpose seating. The trend to larger mini/midibuses in place of earlier van conversions continued with 20 Carlyle bodied Mercedes-Benz 709D for the Solihull network. All the above carried the silver and blue colour scheme from new. The Central Coachways fleet was not overlooked with Bova Futuras, Toyota Coasters with Caetano Optimo bodies and two DAF powered Plaxton 4000 double-deckers. Perhaps surprisingly, the Freight Rover Sherpa re-appeared in the fleet in 1988 when second-hand examples were required for contract gains, particularly in Coventry. With the MCW Metrobus no longer available, West Midlands Travel evaluated a number of options for its future double-deck fleet, resulting in the choice of the Scania N113DRB with Alexander RH bodywork. The 40 examples would be the last new double-deckers for the business until the low floor era. These arrived in the 'red stripe' colour scheme as did the final pre-ESOP additions, five Wright Handybus bodied Dennis Darts.

▶ West Midlands Travel's first new buses had been given a high-profile launch onto what was then considered Birmingham's premier service, the 50, only to be displaced by the Scanias less than three years later. On 23 June 1988, MCW Metrobus Mark 2A 2975 (E975VUK) was seen when new at the Druids Heath terminus ready to work back to Birmingham Central depot at the end of the rush hour. The Mark 2A vehicles were readily distinguishable from the previous Mark 2s by the larger rear windows, clearly seen through the empty vehicle.

◀ West Midlands Travel and MCW celebrated the 1000th Metrobus to be delivered to West Midlands Travel and its predecessors with the numbering of the Metrobus Mark 2A planned to be 2993 (F993XOE) as 1000. In this form it was exhibited at the 1988 Motor Show and entered service as such in Wolverhampton. On 6 May 1989, it had just arrived at the ornate shelters which formed the unloading bays for that city's WMPTE era bus station. The bus would subsequently gain its planned 2993 number and the bus station would be totally remodelled in 2011.

◀ The first of West Midlands Travel's 250 Leyland Lynx arrived early enough to carry F prefix registration plates. One of the earliest, 1074 (F74DDA) was stood against an autumnal backdrop in Dudley bus station on 14 October 1989 en-route for Cradley Heath on former Midland Red service 243.

◀ Most of the Leyland Lynx entered service with G prefix registrations as seen on 1111 (G111EOG) arriving in Birmingham city centre on service 15 from Yardley in April 1990. The split-level entrance step to aid boarding of these vehicles is clearly visible.

23

▲ Passengers shade their eyes from the strong afternoon sun as one of the final Leyland Lynx to enter service, 1312 (G312EOG), loaded in Lower Bull Street Birmingham in August 1990 for a nominally Timesaver 901C journey to Lichfield. This vehicle would be one of those refurbished and remained in service until late in the subsequent Travel West Midlands era. In 2024, Lower Bull Street remains a significant public transport artery with tracks in place for West Midland Metro's Digbeth extension and buses routed in the opposite direction.

The arrival of 20 Mercedes-Benz 709D with Carlyle bodywork in 1990 enabled the upgrade of some of the surviving minibus services, particularly those in the Solihull area. 706 (G706HOP) was seen at the Acocks Green terminus of service Y to Solihull via Yardley on 2 June 1990.

◀ The 40 Alexander RH bodied Scania N113DRB arrived carrying the 'red stripe' colour scheme and were numbered non-consecutively in the 32xx series. This was in response to a DVLC Policy that reserved number plates with common car designations such as 205 and 216 for personalised registration plate purchasers. They entered service on the 50 in Birmingham and 3223 (H223LOM) was seen at The Maypole near the city boundary during November 1990. Competitors on the service turned at this point (and continue to do so in 2024).

◀ Soon after entering service, the Alexander RH bodied Scania N113DRBs had to contend with one of the worst autumn snowfalls that Birmingham had experienced for some years. On 8 December 1990, 3218 (H218LOM) was attempting the climb up Alcester Road past Cocks Moor Wood Leisure Centre whose entrance is blocked by drifting snow. It was part of a convoy of these vehicles returning to depot after services were abandoned for the day, fortunately a Saturday!

◀ Leyland Lynx 1089 (G89EOG) soon appeared in an interim colour scheme with a red stripe at waist level. On a dismal December day in 1990, it was seen descending Birmingham's New Street on the city-centre circuit then followed by many services heading for the south of the city.

▲ Securing the contract for a new network of minibus services serving Cannon Park Shopping Centre in south-west Coventry required additional short-term vehicles including C604KVP, a Freight Rover Sherpa with Carlyle bodywork that had previously operated with Cynon Valley in South Wales. On 23 September 1988, it was seen in the loading bay outside the shopping centre.

▶ Providing an increase in capacity on nominally small bus services in Walsall, the final new vehicles for the arms-length company in August 1991 were five Northern Ireland registered Wright Handybus bodied 9.8m Dennis Darts including 803 (KDZ5803). On 24 March 1992, it was about to depart from the side of Walsall station on a well loaded 331 service to Lodge Farm estate in nearby Willenhall. The open doors clearly show the split step arrangement intended to make access easier for the less able, within five years the concept had been superseded by the arrival of full low floor vehicles.

26

◀ London Country North West was another source of Freight Rover Sherpas with Dormobile bodywork at that time. Their one-time BS14 (D867NVS) was seen in the turning circle at Hamstead on the Birmingham-Sandwell boundary, also on 23 September 1988. It would soon pass to Milton Keynes City Bus.

PART 2
ESOP December 1991

In December 1991, the buyout of West Midlands Travel by its management and employees through an Employee Share Ownership Plan (ESOP) was finalised and new directions began to be explored to service the debt that had been taken on. New vehicle purchases would take a sideline as older vehicles were refurbished and reserve fleet vehicles reactivated to enable more modern vehicles to be hired to operators around the UK. In addition, serious competition was being experienced in several areas of the West Midlands, requiring additional second-hand vehicles, mainly Leyland Nationals, to increase the company's offering.

Competition was reduced through the acquisition of major long-term competitors, two of which would initially be retained as lower-cost units to challenge other competitors. Tame Valley Travel (probably a cover for Drawlane) was, however, closed immediately after acquisition in March 1992, the acquired vehicles going in to store before some were refurbished for the core fleet. Initially retained as subsidiaries were Black Country Buses (formed from the previous Metrowest business) which was established by West Midlands Travel in September 1993, closing in September 1994 and Smiths of Shennington (Your Bus) that followed in December 1993 and was retained into the National Express era. More significant competition was building at that time from Stevensons of Uttoxeter Ltd and the Your Bus operation opened a base in Burton on Trent during 1994 to take the competition to Stevensons' heartland. In September 1994, British Bus acquired the Stevensons business and promptly sold most of the operations but not the vehicles in the West Midlands to West Midlands Travel.

West Midlands Travel vehicles in a myriad of liveries were transferred to the former Stevensons depots in the West Midlands to operate the services while networks were revised and the necessary notice of service changes was given.

Employee-owned West Midlands Travel was also acquisitive outside the West Midlands, adding the Westlink operation from the sale of London Transport's subsidiaries (sold to London United in September 1995), United, TMS and Tees and District from North East Bus and County Bus & Coach in Essex from Lynton Travel (until sold in early 1996 to Cowie Group).

To mark the completion of the ESOP process, each garage received an MCW Metrobus refinished in a celebratory green livery and emboldened with the garage name. A total of 13 vehicles spanning Mark 2 and Mark 2A variants was involved and each was given a 'Limited Edition' label, usually with a number. Encouraging garages' pride in their vehicles, new branding was introduced from late 1994 with a fleetname that prefixed the operating garage with WMBuses. Later, each garage would receive a vehicle in a heritage livery associated with the location.

By 1995, the ESOP business was considering a stock market flotation and the route chosen was a merger with the National Express Group, a business that itself had only relatively recently become publicly listed. The employee shareholders agreed the deal by April. Completion of the merger was a prelude to significant investment and the establishment of a new identity, Travel West Midlands, with a new colour scheme concurrent with the introduction to squadron service of low floor buses in October 1996.

◀ Soon after the launch of the green ESOP buses, Limited Edition No. 1, Dudley Garage's MCW Metrobus Mark 2 2843 (B843AOP) was in the town's bus station on New Year's Eve 1991. Behind it was Wolverhampton Garage's Mark 2A 2993 (F993XOE), the 1000th Metrobus now united with its planned fleet number but devoid of a number on its limited-edition label.

▼ The ESOP vehicles would remain a familiar sight for several years. On 8 June 1993, Limited Edition No. 2, Perry Barr Garage's MCW Metrobus Mark 2 2507 (POG507Y) is passing Birmingham's Bull Ring outbound to Pheasey Estate on the city's boundary with Walsall. The green ESOP buses were also used for the driving challenges in an annual inter-garage 'Rodeo' competition.

2.1 ESOP Vehicle refurbishment

Refurbishing vehicles gained added impetus to maximise the value of investments. Initially this involved the installation of DAF engines into the Leyland National fleet, later many original and Mark 2 MCW Metrobuses would receive a major upgrade including structural work at the rear that changed the appearance of the Mark 2s. Much of this work would be carried out by Marshalls in Cambridge although later examples received less extensive work in house. Some Leyland Nationals would also receive an upgrade with refreshed interiors and Volvo engines including a number of those purchased second hand or taken in from acquired businesses.

▲ In developing the refurbishment process, various options were evaluated to add strength to the body structure at the rear of the MCW Metrobus Mark 2s. These included the abolition of the lower deck rear window on one vehicle (2503 (POG503Y)) or the adoption of a narrow central window as seen here on 2824 (B824AOP) with later branding at Solihull station on 19 November 1996.

◀ Devoid of branding, former Tracline MCW Metrobus Mark 2 2968 (A108WVP) shows signs of refurbishment work including the smaller rear window when loading in Coventry's Broadgate on 14 September 1996. It has also had its electronic destination displays replaced by conventional blinds. This vehicle would become part of the Travel Coventry fleet on the latter's formation and be one of the final three former Tracline vehicles in service with West Midlands Travel. It was one of a large number of MCW Metrobuses sold at auction in 2005 where it attracted the highest bid of the day. It still exists in 2024 as a playbus at an animal sanctuary in Essex.

▼ The standard rear end lower-deck layout for the production Mark 2 Metrobus refurbishments incorporated a window of similar dimensions to the upper-deck one within the original aperture. This was demonstrated by 2774 (B774AOP) in a wet West Bromwich bus station in June 1995 when it carried the later WMBuses branding.

▶ Refurbished Leyland National 1745 (PTF745L) had started life with Ribble some 23 years before it was seen in Birmingham's Navigation Street on 28 September 1996 working service 15 without a destination displayed. It carries WMBuses Perry Barr fleetnames and had come to West Midlands Travel with the Tame Valley Business.

▶ A more radical refurbishment was in store for MCW bodied Leyland Fleetline 6956 (WDA956T). West Midlands Travel, in common with several other operators, had established a need for a more robust small bus to replace midibuses. A solution was seen to be removal of the upper deck from nearly time-served double-deckers and 6956 was West Midlands Travel's first foray in that direction, re-emerging as 1956 and seen with WMBuses Acocks Green fleetnames operating service 42 in Solihull on 19 November 1996. It would remain unique as further conversions were not progressed.

▶ Some of the refreshed Leyland Nationals had the panels either side of the destination screen painted silver, markedly altering their appearance. The concept, which was not perpetuated, was seen on 1805 (OOX805R) at Walsall bus station in January 1996. Subsequent redevelopment has significantly changed the layout of the bus station.

2.2 ESOP New and acquired vehicles

Investment in new vehicles during the ESOP era was limited to a small batch of six Volvo B10Bs with Alexander Strider bodies delivered in 1994. The Volvo chassis found favour though and orders for 150 more but with Wright Endurance bodywork were placed which would be delivered after the National Express merger. In the event, 100 of these would be changed to the low floor equivalent that would introduce the new Travel West Midlands image.

▲ An advance guard for a new generation of single-deck vehicles arrived in 1994, six Alexander Strider bodied Volvo B10Bs whose numbers followed on from the 250 Lynx but with gaps for potential select registrations in the same manner as the Scania double-deckers. They were allocated to Wolverhampton where appropriately registered 1321 (M321LJW) is seen in the bus station carrying the later WMBuses branding on 17 September 1994. This bus would have a short life with West Midlands Travel, being destroyed by fire in 1997.

◀ 1327 (M845OKV), a Wright Endurance bodied Volvo B10B, was initially hired from Volvo in 1995 alongside similar 1328 (N986TWK), both working in the Wolverhampton area. They were added to fleet strength in 1996. On 19 September 1995, an un-numbered and unbranded 1327 took part in that year's Outer Circle Rally, here seen waiting to make the turn from Birmingham's Pebble Mill Road en route for the rally site in Cannon Hill Park. West Midlands Travel's special events heritage vehicle 7225 (MOF225), a Crossley bodied Daimler CVG6, follows. The median strip behind the buses hosted a reserved track tramway until 1952.

▲ From 1995, the Wright bodied Volvo became the brand of choice, initial deliveries included the final full size step-entrance vehicles for West Midlands Travel, 50 Volvo B10Bs with Wright Endurance bodywork. The first of these were also allocated to Wolverhampton where a very new 1332 (N332WOH) with WMBuses branding was seen loading in Lichfield Street on 16 December 1995.

▶ In 1996, West Midlands Travel operated its first low-floor bus in service from West Bromwich garage. 551 (P551EON) was a Volvo B6LE demonstrator with Wright Crusader bodywork to the internal specification of the vehicles ordered by the company, all of which would enter service in a revised colour scheme following the rebranding to Travel West Midlands. In the then standard WMBuses West Bromwich 'red stripe' colour scheme, it was seen on 14 September in one of the layover bays in West Bromwich bus station whilst undertaking short workings to Wednesbury on the 79E service. In 1997 West Midlands Travel acquired it from Volvo.

◀ Transfers of vehicles into the operational parent fleet from the companies acquired nationwide were minimal outside of the Leyland Nationals moved from and returned to Westlink. A need for a higher specification midibus was met by transferring 700 (E290OMG) a Mercedes-Benz 709D with Reeve Burgess Beaver bodywork from County Bus. Amongst the duties it undertook was the Burcot Shuttle, introduced when roadworks on a number of occasions prevented Worcestershire service 145 from serving that village. On 3 August 1996, 700 was waiting in the village to depart on its hourly link to the diverted 145 service on the outskirts of Bromsgrove although often it would run through to the town centre. It carried WMBuses Acocks Green fleetnames, Yardley Wood garage, operator of the 145, loaning the smaller vehicle when needed.

2.3 ESOP Out on hire

Retention of a reserve fleet, predominantly Leyland Fleetlines and Nationals from WMPTE days gave West Midlands Travel the opportunity to make vehicles available on hire to operators across the UK. Maximising the opportunity, in many cases, the vehicles hired-out were modern ones fresh from the operational fleet where they were replaced by reactivated reserve fleet vehicles. Vehicles also moved to the newly acquired subsidiaries both in the West Midlands and beyond.

One of the most significant hire contracts took a substantial number of original MCW Metrobuses and Leyland Nationals to the British Bus operations around Manchester where many received variations on a Bee Line or North Western colour scheme. On 6 May 1995, 2099 (GOG99W-Beeline 790) was seen arriving at Manchester's Piccadilly bus station wearing a conventionally styled Bee Line colour scheme while 2116 (GOG116W-Beeline 791) in Stockport on 31 October 1994 has the more radical diagonal layout. The North Western colour scheme added blue to the mix as seen on 2434 (LOA434X-North Western 801) entered in the 1995 Trans-Lancs Rally at Heaton Park, Manchester on 3 September.

◀ Leyland Nationals also featured in the hires to Bee Line and North Western around Manchester. Their 408, West Midlands Travel's 1479 (TOE497N) carried both companies' fleetnames when seen on a dark afternoon in Manchester during January 1996.

▼ Many hired out vehicles simply gained the new operators name on the original West Midlands Travel colour scheme. Such is the case with MCW Metrobus 2197 (GOG197W) which has branding for Milton Keynes based R&I Buses on its silver based 'red stripe' scheme. In Spring 1994, it was back in Birmingham and was seen in Fazeley Street where it would be steam cleaned under contract prior to its annual certification.

37

▲ Not all hired-out vehicles came directly from the main fleet. Leyland National 1512 (TOE512N) had previously seen service as 114 with the Your Bus subsidiary and on 6 May 1995 was seen in Stockport on hire to Timeline Travel as their 714.

▶ DTC, Darlington Transport Company hired in several West Midlands Travel vehicles as competition in the town intensified, a mix of minibuses and Leyland Fleetlines. 578 (D578NDA) was one of the minibuses which gained DTC colours below the window line, retaining West Midlands Travel grey above. Seen in Darlington town centre on 6 July 1994, its fleet number had been simplified to 78.

◀ Leyland Fleetline 6885 (TVP885S) returned to service in the West Midlands after its hire spell with DTC. On 17 September 1994, it was seen on layover in Wolverhampton bus station in a non-standard grey and blue colour scheme devoid of branding other than its DTC fleet number 214. It carried DTC advertising and a green backed legal lettering panel as normally applied to former Black Country Buses vehicles.

39

▶ A significant proportion of the MCW Metrorider fleet would see hire spells with other operators. Viscount Bus and Coach, Cambus Holdings' Peterborough operation separated out in 1989, operated a number to combat competition from Fen Travel. These included 604 (D604NOE), seen a long way from base in the car park behind Halifax bus station on 7 May 1995.

▶ 632 (D632NOE) was another of the MCW Metroriders to see service with Cambus Holdings who operated them on behalf of the hirer, Cambridge City Council. Painted green and yellow, they provided a shoppers' service around the centre of Cambridge until replaced by new Optare Metroriders. On 632's return to the West Midlands, it re-entered service without being repainted, just WMBuses West Bromwich fleetnames being applied. It was seen in that town's bus station on 3 August 1996.

▶ MCW Metrorider 628 (D628NOE) would gain a cream and blue colour scheme while working for Pennine Blue, a scheme it would initially retain along with the Lady Penelope name when returned to service at West Bromwich in October 1994 following the takeover of the Stevenson's operations. Carrying a liberal coating of road dirt, it was seen departing from West Bromwich bus station soon after its return.

40

In 1995, several vehicles were given a dark green colour scheme for short-term operation with Buckinghamshire Road Car on a free service sponsored by Marks and Spencer to their new store in Milton Keynes. After return to the West Midlands, two of the Reeve-Burgess bodied Dodge S56s involved would subsequently be revived, retaining the green colour scheme, to operate a Christmas 1995 Park and Ride service in Wolverhampton. 581 (D581NDA) was one and was seen looking for custom in a bleak Victoria Square on 22 December 1995. Note the incorrectly installed number blinds!

▲ West Midlands Travel was the successful bidder for the first London Buses unit to be sold. Stanwell Buses, trading as Westlink, had been a nominally lower-cost operation around Kingston and Heathrow using mainly midibuses and Leyland Nationals. To add capacity, West Midlands Travel drafted a number of MCW Metrobus Mark 2s from the parent fleet including 2879 (B879DOM) seen on service 411 in Kingston on 11 March 1995. It would return to Birmingham after the subsidiary was sold on and remained in service with West Midlands Travel/National Express until 2009.

41

▶ Following the acquisition of North East Bus (formerly the northern part of Caldaire Holdings), a significant number of Leyland Nationals moved to Teesside where they operated in colour schemes ranging from standard West Midlands Travel 'red stripe' to the full local schemes. In Stockton-on-Tees on 22 January 1996, 1525 (TOE525N – TMS 3653) was seen with just TMS fleetnames added while TMS 3657 (VOD 601S) had been given a blue stripe variant, presumably on a full repaint as this was one of the vehicles acquired from Midland Red West. Leyland National 2 1040 (DOC40V – Tees 3750) had received the full Tees red and yellow colour scheme by the time it was seen in Middlesborough on 4 May 1996.

2.4 Central Coachways evolves

WMPTE's initial foray into minibus operation in 1985 took place using the Central Coachways business prior to the adoption of specific minibus terms and conditions at Deregulation. The second incarnation of Central Coachways as a bus business commenced with a pair of contract services in 1993. Using premises at Miller Street, Birmingham, a variety of minibuses and Leyland Nationals were painted in the plain blue colour scheme and put to work on contracts and commercial routes competing, mainly, with City Buslines, a company formed by former West Midlands Travel managers. In summer 1994, the Central Coachways bus operation was disbanded at short notice and the remaining routes moved to existing West Midlands Travel garages. On the coaching side, the London Liner service would be discontinued and operations on the National Express network increased with a dedicated fleet in National Express white.

▲ Investment in the Central Coachways fleet during the arms-length years included a pair of DAF SBR3000 tri-axles with Plaxton Paramount 4000 coachwork branded for the London Liner service. On 8 September 1990, G776HOV was seen on Colmore Row in Birmingham city centre.

◀ Robin Hood bodied Iveco TurboDaily 49-10 591 (D591NDA) was one of several of the batch of minibuses originally used on the Solihull network to transfer to Central Coachways. On 2 September 1994, it was seen emerging from Birmingham's Brunel Street with the Brutalist New Street Station signalbox to its right. Now a listed building, it is no longer operational following the opening of the West Midlands Signalling Centre at Saltley.

▲ At almost the same location on the same day, Reeve-Burgess bodied Dodge S56 581 (D581NDA) was working for Central Coachways on route N76. A hastily scribbled on sheet of paper serves as a minimalist destination indicator, one step in advance of the totally blank Iveco.

▶ Some Central Coachways bus services were provided with full destination blinds, here displayed on Leyland National 1011 (AOL11T) on service 43 to Hall Green. On 2 September 1994, it was seen in Birmingham's Navigation Street, once a major hub of the bus network but in 2024 served only by West Midlands Metro trams that cross to the rear of the bus in a location otherwise unchanged by redevelopment.

44

◀ National Express established the Rapide concept to add additional finesse including hostess service to key links on its network. The Black Country to London route was one chosen with vehicles provided by West Midlands Travel through Central Coachways. On 8 May 1993, fully branded Bova Futura G543JOG was seen entering Dudley bus station in the shadow of Dudley Castle bound for London.

45

▶ In 1993, National Express developed the Expressliner 2 concept with Plaxton and Volvo for standard vehicles to be used across its network. West Midlands Travel were early adopters of the concept, taking a batch of the Premiere 3500 bodied B10Ms including 8002 (K2CEN) which was seen outbound from Birmingham to Aberystwyth on 8 May 1993.

▼ By the 1995 Sandwell Rally held on 14 May, West Midlands Travel was marketing a joint WM Holidays and Smiths Coaches tour programme. The former MCW prototype Metroliner 400GT 1932 (D932ODA), devoid of most of its London Liner branding and with additional red and silver stripes was used to promote the product at the event. Note the colourful WMHolidays' T-shirt worn by the driver.

46

2.5 Replacing the Stevensons operations

The growth of the Stevensons operation across the West Midlands and out into neighbouring counties provided a significant challenge to West Midlands Travel although eventually the growth appeared to become unsustainable and the Stevensons business was sold to British Bus in summer 1994. Rapidly an agreement was put in place whereby West Midlands Travel would acquire the two Black Country depots and the majority of services including those into Worcestershire and south Staffordshire, British Bus retaining a number in the east of the conurbation. West Midlands Travel's competing Your Bus operation in Burton-on-Trent was also discontinued. Very few operational vehicles were involved in the transaction resulting in the transfer or reactivation of West Midlands Travel vehicles in a myriad of colour schemes. Many had hastily applied fleetnames and legal lettering, often on mismatched coloured vinyl and all needed to carry 'on hire to Stevensons of Uttoxeter Ltd' notices in the windscreen until service revisions and de/re-registrations were concluded

◀ Following the acquisition of Stanwell Buses from London Buses, a batch of short length (10.3m) Leyland Nationals were transferred to the West Midlands. They were renumbered in the 19xx series following on from similar vehicles in the Black Country Buses fleet unlike other acquired Leyland Nationals that received numbers in the 1xxx series that usually matched their registration marks. On 23 August 1994, 1907 (BYW373V), former London Buses LS373 was seen in Birmingham's New Street still in Westlink colours with a makeshift destination board and legal lettering on a green vinyl.

▲ Double-deckers were required for a small number of the Stevensons services and some Your Bus Leyland Atlanteans were used in the very short term. MCW bodied Leyland Fleetline FE30 6999 (WDA999T) looks to have been reactivated to cover the duties and is seen in Wolverhampton bus station on 17 September 1994 with the obligatory 'on hire' sticker. It has a makeshift destination blind and displays no fleetnumbers or current fleetname. It had last been used on hire to the Darlington Transport Company.

47

▶ Latterly used by Central Coachways and retaining that operation's blue colour scheme, Robin Hood bodied Iveco TurboDaily 49-10 587 (D587NDA) had gained the latest WMBuses West Bromwich fleetname and legal lettering on a green vinyl when seen in that town's bus station on 15 October 1994.

▼ As it entered West Bromwich bus station on 12 December 1994, Leyland National 1467 (ROK467M) highlighted the transitional nature of the fleet in the immediate post Stevensons period. It carries the Your Bus colour scheme, a fleet number that would relate to a hire spell elsewhere, the then current WMBuses Walsall fleetname on a silver vinyl and a Hartshill (by then closed) allocation label in the windscreen!

▲ Stevensons operated several services into Worcestershire and these would bring West Midlands Travel buses back to places such as Bromsgrove on a regular basis. In the bus station there on 27 August 1994 was MCW Metrorider 677 (F677YOG), one of a number that had been operated by Black Country Buses and still carrying the green Metrowest colour scheme. A week later, Your Bus Plaxton Pointer bodied Dennis Dart D84 (J348GKH) was on the same departure. The 202 service is basically unchanged in 2024 but is now operated by Diamond Bus. It principally serves suburban areas in the south Birmingham conurbation but outside the city boundary.

2.6 Rebranding to WMBuses

From late 1994, West Midlands Travel adopted revised branding across its fleet, operations now being more stable following the cessation of operation by some significant competitors. Buses received a new fleetname of their home garage name prefixed by WMBuses on the standard 'red stripe' colour scheme. Most garages would also receive a vehicle repainted in a livery appropriate to their former local municipal undertaking. The subsidiary Your Bus operation would be branded WM YOURBUS in the previous Your Bus style script.

▶ MCW bodied Leyland Fleetline 6477 (NOC477R) displayed the WMBuses West Bromwich fleetname as it turned from Corporation Street into Bull Street, Birmingham on 23 September 1994. It is one of the Fleetlines given a revised Webasco cab heating and demisting system in WMPTE days that did away with the grilles on the front. Emphasising the frequency of services along Birmingham's Soho Road, the Fleetline on the 74 is followed by a Wolverhampton Metrobus on the 79.

▲ At Deregulation, Midland Red West introduced a series of services in the 8x range that left Birmingham city centre along the Bristol Road. By Autumn 1995, West Midlands Travel were providing the Sunday 83 service along that corridor, using Leyland Lynx from Quinton garage. On 22 October 1995, 1312 (G312EOG) displayed its WMBuses Quinton fleetname as it passed the junction of Eastern Road with Bristol Road in Edgbaston. The autumnal trees mark the road's central reservation which hosted tram tracks until 1952. A cycle way has subsequently been installed, fortunately with minimal loss of vegetation.

◀ WMBuses Perry Barr fleetnames are carried by refreshed Leyland National 1731 (VNO731S) arriving in Birmingham city centre on 5 April 1996. It was new to Eastern National and came to West Midlands Travel through the Black Country Buses subsidiary. It has revised lights and a redesigned front bumper. Unlike some other refreshed Leyland Nationals, it retains the black panels either side of the number and destination screen which just displays a route number, suggesting the vehicle is out on loan.

◀ The blue on MCW bodied Leyland Fleetline 6935 (WDA935T) has faded significantly in places, emphasising the size of vinyl required to replace the previous West Midlands Travel fleetname with a WMBuses Coventry one. On 10 August 1995, it was passing Swanswell gate when leaving Coventry city centre bound for Wood End. The buildings in the background have subsequently been swept away but the gate still stands in 2024.

◀ Free Christmas Park and Ride services operated to several parking lots around Wolverhampton in 1995. That to the south of the city centre appeared to be attracting little custom as a pair of WMBuses Wolverhampton branded Volvo Citybuses with Alexander P type bodies, led by 1056 (C56HOM), waited in Bilston Street on 16 December. By 2024, the supermarket building behind the buses which incorporated the spired tower had been closed for several years.

51

The garage in Liverpool Street, Birmingham Central, was simply referred to as Central in the WMBuses era. Here it is carried by MCW Metrobus Mark 2 2960 (D960NDA), recently refreshed into the standard 'red stripe' colour scheme from its Timesaver colours. It retained its high back seating and was still working a limited stop service as it departed Birmingham for Coventry on 23 July 1994.

▲ An unexpected outcome of vehicle reactivation in the 1990s was the appearance of several Coventry ordered East Lancs bodied Daimler or Leyland Fleetlines at Walsall, a garage that had lost its Fleetline allocation several years previously. With correct WMBuses Walsall branding, 6723 (NOC723R) was seen loading in the WMPTE incarnation of the town's bus station before departing on the former trolleybus service to Mossley on 3 August 1996.

▲ Birmingham's Stephenson Place was once part of a major bus corridor, in 2024 the only public transport in the area is provided by West Midlands Metro. Displaying WMBuses Hockley fleetnames, former Tracline MCW Metrobus Mark 2 2974 (A114WVP) passed through on 23 July 1995. It had lost its electronic destination displays for standard blinds.

53

▲ The new WMBuses Washwood Heath panel on MCW bodied Leyland Fleetline 6898 (TVP898S) has failed to cover the marks left from the removal of its previous vinyl and it also shows sign of being painted around the advertising it carried at the time of repaint. On 13 July 1996, it was on the hump above pedestrian subways at the junction of Corporation Street and Bull Street in Birmingham, a feature subsequently swept away and later remodelled again with a triangular junction for West Midland Metro tram lines.

▶ Acquired with the Smiths of Shennington (Your Bus) business were six Dennis Darts with Plaxton Pointer bodywork bought new by that company in 1992/3. To meet the need for more robust smaller vehicles initially planned to be Fleetlines converted to single-deck, these were transferred to the main fleet in 1995 and repainted in the 'red stripe' colour scheme. In early January 1995, 1997 (J997UAC) was seen on the service 32 stand in Shirley Road, Acocks Green, carrying WMBuses Acocks Green fleetnames. It would transfer to Wolverhampton as 811, later moving to Travel Dundee as number 30.

◀ On the closure of Central Coachways bus operation, service 44 to the south of Birmingham was transferred to Yardley Wood Garage and converted to minibus operation, bringing the Carlyle bodied Mercedes-Benz 0709D to Birmingham city centre on a regular basis. Displaying WMBuses Yardley Wood fleetnames but still to lose its previous Acocks Green allocation sticker on the windscreen, 703 (G703HOP) was seen in New Street, Birmingham on 24 August 1994.

▶ MCW Metrobus 2102 (GOG102W) demonstrated the WMBuses Lea Hall fleetname when departing Birmingham's Bull Ring bound for Chelmsley Wood on 5 August 1995. Prior to refurbishment, this vehicle had been the first in the WMPTE fleet to carry an electronic destination display.

▶ In preparation for the first low-floor midibuses which would occupy the number series from 501 upwards, the Carlyle bodied Mercedes-Benz 709Ds were renumbered in the 2xx series. On 27 July 1996, 204 (previously 704 – G704HOP) carrying WMBuses Acocks Green fleetnames was seen passing the Big Bulls Head in Digbeth, Birmingham, working service 650, a Centro contracted service aimed to bring more of south Birmingham's inner suburban streets closer to a bus route.

▶ Some of the vehicles reactivated for the takeover of the Stevensons operations would remain in service from West Bromwich garage, including Robin Hood bodied Iveco TurboDaily 49-10 596 (D596NDA) which was seen on 7 September 1996 with a short working between West Bromwich and Wednesbury as service 79E, a route that was also home to West Midlands Travel's first low floor bus at the time.

56

2.7 WMBuses – recognising its heritage

▲ Birmingham City Transport liveried MCW Metrobus Mark 2A 3043 (F43XOF) was Lea Hall garage's heritage liveried vehicle. On 5 April 1996, it was seen in the slip road outside Birmingham's Moor Street Station that was provided when the city's ringway was built in the 1960s. The road, together with the pub and goods depot behind the bus were swept away by further development in the early 2000s and 3043's position would now be inside the Selfridges store.

◀ In Birmingham City Transport colours, 3050 (F50XOF) operated from Washwood Heath garage and was seen in Birmingham's Bull Street on a dull day in May 1996 loading for a service 55 journey to Kingshurst.

57

A few minutes after the image of 3043, Hockley Garage's example, MCW Metrobus Mark 2A 3088 (F88XOF) was seen just a few metres away, still within the footprint of the current Selfridges store, heading through the Bull Ring bound for Great Barr on service 16A. In 2024, the core National Express West Midlands 16 service follows the same route to Great Barr, the 16A being used by Diamond Bus for journeys diverting to West Bromwich.

▲ When they were first refinished, it was not unusual to find a selection of the heritage liveried vehicles at local bus rallies. At the 1996 Sandwell Rally on 11 May, Birmingham City Transport liveried MCW Metrobus Mark2A 3030 (F30XOF) was entered by the Perry Barr garage team where it was flanked by Yardley Wood garage's 2856 and Birmingham Central garage's 3225.

▲ Only two MCW Metrobus Mark 2s gained the Birmingham City Transport heritage livery, one being Quinton garage based 2872 (B872DOM) seen here in early August 1996 in Navigation Street, Birmingham working service 103, one of a number of radial services to be given a circular route around Birmingham city centre under the 'Centrelink' title, partially replacing the Centrebus service that had been rendered impracticable by ongoing pedestrianisation of the city centre.

59

▶ The West Bromwich Corporation Transport livery of the 1950s with gold lining was the most complex applied by West Midlands Travel, the recipient being MCW Metrobus Mark 2A 3033 (F33XOF). The livery was shown most advantageously under a clear blue sky in West Bromwich's WMPTE era bus station on 14 September 1996.

▼ The late 1950s style Coventry Corporation Transport heritage livery applied to MCW Metrobus 2 2867 would be long-lived, surviving into the Travel Coventry era. On 17 July 1996, it was turning into the city's Trinity Street headed for Leamington on the 12 service which serves the University of Warwick on the city's southern boundary. The background architecture is unchanged in 2024 but the road layout in the foreground is now a shared space, principally for pedestrians and buses.

60

◀ 'Odd one out' amongst the heritage liveried vehicles was Alexander RH bodied Scania N113DRB 3225 (H225LON) which was painted in Birmingham City Transport colours for Birmingham Central Garage. It was an appropriate choice given that West Midlands Travel's special event heritage vehicle was a Crossley bodied Daimler CVG6, 7225 (MOF225), formerly Birmingham City Transport 3225. The Scania was often used on the 777 shuttle service to the Riva Bingo Club in Birmingham's Bath Row on which it was descending Stephenson Place on 21 September 1996.

◀ Early MCW Metrobus Mark 2A 2989 (E989VUK) was selected to carry a Wolverhampton Corporation Transport heritage livery, the style chosen being that carried by vehicles from the 1940s and 1950s. With large expanses of yellow, it certainly brightened up Wolverhampton's bus station on a dull 17 February 1996.

◀ The immediate pre-WMPTE livery style used by Walsall Corporation Transport was chosen for the Walsall garage heritage vehicle, a lighter blue with thin yellow bands although the finish, at least initially, appeared glossier than its forebears. After nearly a year in service, the upper-deck is still shiny but the arduous local conditions have had an impact on the lower panels' appearance. On 9 November 1996, it was working the 334 service from Walsall's Bradford Place on an indirect route to Wolverhampton.

PART 3
Contracts and route branding

◀ An early attempt to upgrade Birmingham's Outer Circle service 11 involved the deployment from Perry Barr garage of Leyland Nationals in the then current colour scheme complete with bold Outer Circle branding on the sides, it was short lived. In February 1988, Leyland National 2 1032 (DOC32V) was on the stand outside the B&Q superstore at the Fox and Goose crossing in Washwood Heath. The graffiti tag below the driver's window was not part of the route branding!

▶ New Invention is a suburb of Walsall west of the M6 motorway and to the north of Willenhall. Its location adds logic to the layout of the route branding details carried on MCW Metrobus 2 2642 (ROX642Y) which emphasises the suburb's connection to both Walsall and Willenhall, two locations otherwise linked by much faster direct services. On 9 September 1988, 2642 was awaiting a short working to New Invention from Park Street in Walsall, an area pedestrianised a few years later. A similar service is still run by National Express West Midlands in 2024 but has reverted to its pre-WMPTE service number, 41.

◀ Strictly not branded for a specific route, many buses operating services to the growing shopping mall on the former Round Oak Steelworks site at Merry Hill gained an appropriate strapline in the early 1990s. 'Your Way to the Merry Hill Centre' would have been somewhat of a misnomer on MCW Metrobus 2058 (BOK58V) when seen leaving Dudley bus station on 18 March 1993 bound for Wednesbury on the one time Midland Red service 245. Brierley Hill High Street will have been the closest point to Merry Hill it had passed through, a significant walk away.

▲ Route branding meets all-over-advertising on MCW Metrobus Mark 2 2748 (A748WVP) which was given a sides and rear wrap promoting service 8 in 1994. The simple snooker-based concept is clearly seen as the vehicle waited in Alcester Street Birmingham having just completed an 8E short working to the nearby Pershore Road junction on 3 August 1994. Note the early use of WMBuses Central as a fleetname.

63

▲ Birmingham's International Conference Centre (ICC) opened early in 1991, managed alongside other city venues including the NEC. In readiness for the opening, a contract for Park and Ride services was let to West Midlands Travel for which the company converted several of its newer Leyland Nationals to dual-door standee specifications. In advance of the ICC opening, Mark 1 1017 (AOL17T) was at the NEC for the Travel show on 5 January 1991, displaying both NEC branding and advertising for West Midlands Travel's own holiday stand within the show.

▶ A later use for several of the dual-door Leyland National Mark 2 conversions was on the Town Centre Bus in Wolverhampton (where City status was not achieved until 2001). Occasionally, these would be called upon to operate regular services and on 1 February 1994, 1025 (DOC25V) had arrived in Dudley bus station.

◀ Most of the Leyland Nationals converted to dual-door standee specification were 11.9m Mark2s including 1039 (DOC39V) seen with full ICC branding at the rear of the building on 5 March 1991.

65

▶ For the Wolverhampton council sponsored free bus, the Leyland National Mark 2s received standard 'red stripe' colours on the front panel, full West Midlands Travel fleetnames and bold Town Centre Bus vinyls. On its designated service, 1042 (DOC42V) displayed all these features as it emerged from Lichfield Street in central Wolverhampton on 9 July 1994.

▶ In preparation for a new focus on colour coded route branding, many vehicles started to receive diagonal colour bands during early 1996. On 3 August 1996, refurbished Hockley based MCW Metrobus Mark 2 2546 (POG546Y) has received a lime green stripe which will eventually gain details for the service it is working, the 101, which had been extended in a loop around Birmingham city centre to incorporate the Centrebus service. In 2024, the 101 penetrates the city centre no further than Colmore Row. Similarly finished 2683 (A683UOE) was passing it in Corporation Street, Birmingham.

▶ MCW Metrobuses on Acocks Green operated service 1 gained route branding on a mauve diagonal band with the '1 – the one' tagline added. 2605 (POG605Y), one of the vehicles involved, was seen in Brunel Street, Birmingham on 21 September 1996. At the time, service 1 operated into the city centre, subsequently it reverted to terminating at Five Ways with the city bound frequency later reduced as alternate buses were diverted to the Queen Elizabeth Hospital.

PART 4
Special events, visitors and demonstrators

◀ After being the only vehicle to be operational as a PSV throughout the WMPTE era, open-top former Birmingham City Transport Park Royal bodied Daimler Fleetline CRG6 3867 (NOV867G) continued on special duties with West Midlands Travel, including undertaking a goodwill visit to Dublin. It had gained a grey based colour scheme by 5 January 1991 when it was part of the company's presence at the Travel Show held at the NEC. Alongside was former WMPTE Daimler Fleetline 4261 (EOF261L) that passed to City of Birmingham Leisure Services relatively early in its life as an open-topper following a de-roofing event.

▶ A new open-top vehicle for special events was created by West Midlands Travel in 1994. Based on MCW Metrobus 2028 (BOK28V), it was finished in a colourful self-promotional scheme that retained fleet colours on the front upper deck panels. On 10 July 1994, it was shown to the public in the Aston Villa car park adjacent to the then Aston Manor Road Transport Museum which is in the background. The latter closed in 2011 and relocated to Aldridge.

67

▶ Park Royal bodied Daimler Fleetline 4069 (YOX69K) was converted to open-top in WMPTE days and passed to West Midlands Travel in that guise. It was still in use for special events in 1994 having gained the 'red stripe' colour scheme and WMBuses Wolverhampton branding. On 28 August 1994, it was operating additional journeys on the 1c service in conjunction with an open day at Acocks Green garage.

At the Acocks Green garage open day on 23 July 1995, visitors had the opportunity to sample vehicles from two of West Midlands Travel's recently acquired subsidiaries working additional journeys on service 1. From Westlink came Leyland Titan TN15 T265 (GYE265W), seen emerging from the Acocks Green garage building. Townlink in Harlow provided M267VPU, a Dennis Lancet LLF with low floor Wright bodywork. Possibly the first low floor vehicle to operate in the West Midlands, it was seen at the Shirley Road terminus of service 1 in Acocks Green.

▶ For the 1996 open day at Acocks Green garage on 28 July, Tees and District Optare Prisma bodied Mercedes-Benz O405 3004 (M304SAJ) was one of the guest visitors to operate additional journeys on service 1. It was seen leaving the garage in conditions typical of the day.

▶ West Midlands Travel inspected a large number of demonstration vehicles, several being subjected to evaluation in regular service. One of the earliest comparison trials in 1987 involved Leyland and Scania vehicles and took place on service 71 between Solihull and Sutton Coldfield. Leyland provided its latest Lynx demonstrator, representing the on-going development of the model from the evaluation vehicles WMPTE acquired in 1985. Scania sourced a recent East Lancs bodied Scania K92CRB D163WTV from Kettlewells of Retford for the duration of the trial and it was seen in summer 1987 on the outskirts of Chelmsley Wood. The Lynx found favour. **JW**

▶ Before placing the order for 40 new Scania double-deckers, West Midlands Travel evaluated an example destined for Nottingham City Transport, an early user of the N113DRB model with Alexander RH bodywork. During its stay, 380 (F380JTV) was a regular performer on the 82 service along Birmingham's Dudley Road, a service on which it was seen in Birmingham's Navigation Street on 18 October 1989. It carried Nottingham legal lettering but no branding for that city's arms-length operation.

On 22 September 1988, Carlyle's Iveco TurboDaily 49-10 based Dailybus demonstrator E486ONX was on the forecourt of Lea Hall garage. This was an early station on its round of demonstrations across the UK which included two spells with Midland Red West. In the mid-1990s, it would be acquired by West Midlands Travel and put in to service in the 'red stripe' colour scheme as WMBuses Acocks Green 7486. It carried 486 as a fleetnumber when seen on the 145 Burcot Shuttle in Bromsgrove on 9 September 1996.

▶ In 1990, West Midlands Travel evaluated Optare Delta demonstrator G837LWR on service 35, a WMPTE creation that brought together three feeder services in Birmingham's southern suburbs, giving them a direct link to the city centre. It was seen in Hallam Street at the core of densely populated Balsall Heath on 28 July 1990. No orders were elicited for the DAF based Delta despite the widespread use of DAF engines by West Midlands Travel to repower Leyland Nationals. Smiths of Shennington (Your Bus) did however acquire five of the model in 1990 and these would pass with that operation to West Midlands Travel.

Repainted MCW Metrobus Mark 2 2878 (B878DOM) carrying WMBuses Perry Barr fleetnames was provided to Valetmatic to demonstrate their Trident bus washer at Coach and Bus 1995, held at the NEC on 12 October 1995.

PART 5
The ancillary fleet

West Midlands Travel took over several ancillary vehicles from WMPTE at its formation including Foden heavy recovery units, training vehicles and the Leyland National promotions unit. These would gain a variety of liveries with the company and be joined by additional vehicles, particularly for training purposes following the establishment of TRAN-SKIL, a training company joint venture.

One of the more unexpected acquisitions by West Midlands Travel to support its training activities was 8658 (ARN658C), an MCW bodied Leyland PD3A/1 previously Preston Bus 73 that arrived in the all-over yellow that it had carried with Lonsdale Coaches in Lancashire. It was later repainted white with blue wings and both West Midlands Travel and TRAN-SKIL logo. Lea Hall garage forecourt was a regular location to find training buses and 8658 was seen there in yellow on 13 September 1988. The following year on 29 July and now in white, it was entering Dudley Bus Station with a trainee at the wheel and the instructor leaning through the opening at the rear of the cab where the staircase had been removed. The raised instructor's seat is clearly visible. West Midlands Travel also acquired a former Brighton Corporation Leyland PD2 for training purposes.

73

▶ Transferred as a promotional vehicle from WMPTE, dual-door Leyland National 1792 (KOM792P) would undergo a number of branding iterations in support of West Midlands Travel. By 14 May 1989 when it attended that year's Sandwell Rally, it was in a silver-based scheme complete with a giant telephone handset on the roof and bee motifs. If it was intended to promote telephone contact with the company, it is perhaps surprising that the contact number is not that prominent... Later it was painted in a variation of the 'red stripe' colour scheme with yellow in place of silver, the telephone handset was removed and a substantial awning added to the nearside which the weather conditions at the 1996 Acocks Green open day on 28 July appear to have defeated.

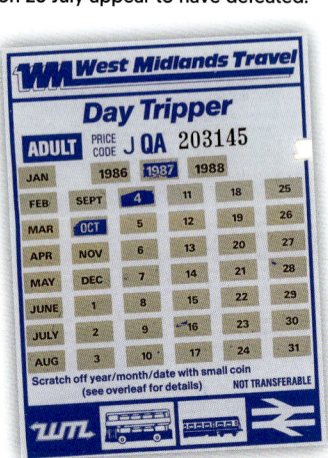

◀ Before vehicle recovery became almost exclusively the domain of specialists, most larger bus operators would have at least one heavy recovery vehicle, either purpose built, like the Fodens transferred to West Midlands Travel from WMPTE or converted from military type vehicles. In the latter category is Birmingham Central's Bedford MK 108 (Q233VOE) seen heading into the city centre on 23 June 1989.

◀ Looking no different externally to when it was in public service as 6493, MCW bodied Leyland Fleetline FE30 8493 (NOC493R) would have been in use by TRAN-SKIL as a training vehicle when seen on the forecourt of Lea Hall garage on 1 August 1989. It has an allocation sticker for the distant HartsHill garage.

◀ WMPTE's standard heavy duty recovery vehicle was the three axle Foden and 102 (Q76VOE) was one that transferred to West Midlands Travel. By the time it participated in the 1993 Sandwell Parade and Rally on 9 May, it had gained the 'red stripe' colour scheme as West Bromwich garage's recovery vehicle.

75

▲ West Midlands Travel also employed two-axle Foden recovery vehicles including 105 (Q79 VOE) seen in Dudley bus station on 12 November 1993. It carried a bespoke application of West Midlands Travel's colour scheme and a plastic Red Nose, this being evidence of support for TV's Comic Relief fundraising event 'Red Nose Day.' The Comic Relief charity was founded by Lenny Henry and Richard Curtis in 1985.

▶ 416 (C816CBU) was a Dodge S56 with Northern Counties bodywork which West Midlands Travel acquired with the Tame Valley Travel business and placed into store. The former GMPTE vehicle returned to home territory when it went out on loan to Pennine Blue in Dukinfield. Returning to Birmingham, it gained a non-standard variation on the 'red stripe' colour scheme and was put to work as an ancillary vehicle at Yardley Wood garage. On 26 September 1994, it was seen attending to street infrastructure on Stratford Road in Sparkbrook.

◀ On 3 January 1990, a Carlyle bodied Iveco 49-10 was in use by the TRAN-SKIL organisation when seen in a bleak and remarkably traffic free New Street in Birmingham. New as a Carlyle demonstrator in 1988, 8511 (E511TOV) would later enter operational service with West Midlands Travel at West Bromwich in the 'red stripe' colour scheme as 7511. In between it had seen hire spells with operators including Flexibus in Belfast and People's Provincial.

WAYFARER III USER GUIDE
(ON-BUS EQUIPMENT)
FEBRUARY 1990

West Midlands Travel

PART 6
All over advertising

◀ HartsHill based MCW Metrobus 2142 (GOG142W) transferred from WMPTE in the Lex Mead advertising livery it was carrying in Dudley bus station on 21 March 1987. It had carried no fleetname in WMPTE days and now only the new legal lettering panel shows evidence of West Midlands Travel ownership.

◀ The Coventry Building Society continues to be a strong financial organisation in 2024 while building a national presence. In 1988, its reputation was more local and the introduction of cashpoint cards was a major event in improving its customers' access to their money. Their availability was promoted on Coventry based MCW Metrobus 2167 (GOG167W), seen leaving Pool Meadow bus station on 23 March 1988.

◀ America came to Birmingham with Jefferson's Restaurant and Bar which opened in Hagley Road, Quinton. An all-over-advertising scheme featuring icons of the southern USA was applied to MCW Metrobus 2400 (LOA400X) from nearby Quinton garage to promote it. WMPTE had extended Birmingham City Transport's 9 service from Quinton to Stourbridge so 2400, seen here near Halesowen bus station on 21 May 1988, would have passed the restaurant in the course of its journey into the city.

◀ With the decline of manufacturing in the Black Country, tourism was seen as a partial replacement promoted heavily by Dudley Metropolitan Borough at the end of the 20th Century. Many of the local attractions featured in the all-over-advertising scheme applied to Dudley based MCW Metrobus Mark 2 2703 (A703UOE) which was seen departing from Birmingham on 27 May 1988, bound for Langley, it would pass none of them en route!

◀ Before the widespread development of digital television and broadband, additional TV channel entertainment required either a satellite receiver or a dedicated cable connection. Many cable networks were installed in densely populated areas including Coventry and that city's local network advertised itself on MCW Metrobus 2158 (GOG158W), seen in Pool Meadow bus station on 27 September 1988.

79

▶ Several MCW Metroriders gained all-over-advertising at the peak of minibus operation including 607 (D607NOE) which was decorated to the requirements of Wolverhampton Metropolitan Borough to advertise its local markets. On 21 October 1988, it was setting down a fair load of passengers in Wolverhampton bus station. With the exception of the bridge railings in the background, the whole area around the vehicle is unrecognisable in 2024.

▼ Another MCW Metrorider to carry an all-over-advert was 679 (F679YOG) seen in Cradley on 25 March 1989. Coalite developed as a home improvements business in the Black Country during the 1980s and probably sold the smokeless fuel marketed under the 'Coalite' brand that remains available today.

80

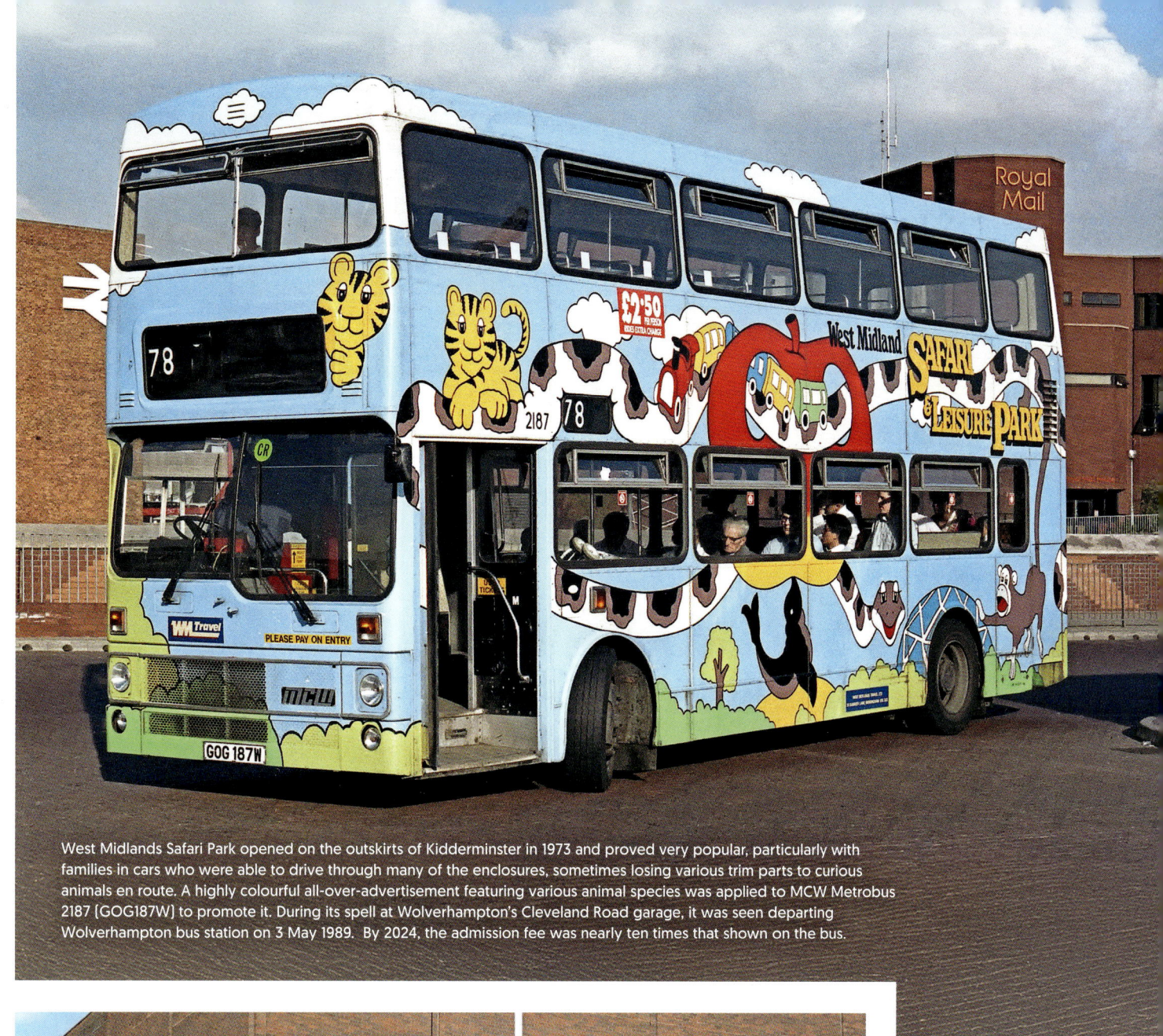

West Midlands Safari Park opened on the outskirts of Kidderminster in 1973 and proved very popular, particularly with families in cars who were able to drive through many of the enclosures, sometimes losing various trim parts to curious animals en route. A highly colourful all-over-advertisement featuring various animal species was applied to MCW Metrobus 2187 (GOG187W) to promote it. During its spell at Wolverhampton's Cleveland Road garage, it was seen departing Wolverhampton bus station on 3 May 1989. By 2024, the admission fee was nearly ten times that shown on the bus.

◀ Grattan, the Bradford based catalogue retailer founded in 1912 and still operational online in 2024, operated several what would now be called outlet stores under the Manorgrove brand. The West Midlands one was advertised on MCW Metrobus 2217 (GOG217W), seen in Station Street, Walsall on 13 May 1989. It was using the tight turning circle that was created following pedestrianisation of parts of Walsall town centre.

81

▲ Creating that holiday ambiance, MCW Metrobus Mark 2 2469 (NOA469X) was given a scheme for HCI 'all-inclusive' holidays complete with palm trees, sun, sand and blue skies. In April 1990, it brightened up Birmingham's Bull Ring while working from Birmingham Central garage on service 50.

▶ West Midlands Travel initially continued the operation of Birmingham's 101 Centrebus service until advancing pedestrianisation limited its access to the city centre. The 1980 delivered short Leyland National 2s carrying all-over-advertising remained the vehicle of choice for it. On 24 June 1989, 1049 (DOC49V) was turning into New Street past Waterstone's bookshop which is still trading there in 2024 but now facing a much-enlarged pedestrianised area.

◀ In 1989, Birmingham celebrated its centenary as a city, an event marked by a colourful wrap on newly delivered MCW Metrobus Mark 2A 3068 (F68XOF). The wrap started with a horse-tram on the front nearside continuing through trams and trolleybuses to the city's buses, not forgetting Midland Red, and finished after the current Metrobus with a vision for the future that has yet to be realised. On 22 July 1989, the Birmingham Central garage based vehicle was covering for a dual-purpose example on the 963 Timesaver service to the city boundary at Gannow near Rubery.

83

▲ An abstract background in autumnal colours was chosen for the Barclays Bank advertising on MCW Metrobus Mark 2 2629 (ROX629Y). On 27 July 1990, it appears to have had a recent change of garage and was working service 6 to the south of Birmingham despite the DY (Dudley) garage code on the windscreen.

▶ One Stop is a shopping centre hemmed in between the A34 Walsall Road, Perry Barr railway station and the river Tame in north Birmingham. It has undergone a number of iterations over the years, underpinned by a major Asda store that had relocated from Aston Villa FC's parking area. Perry Barr Garage's MCW Metrobus Mark 2 2653 (ROX653Y) carried an all-over-advert for it when seen at the Kingstanding terminus of service 33 in June 1991. Note that the balloon motifs carried the names of the stores that could be experienced there.

◀ Wraparound (Polybus) adverts were used again in the 1990s to promote West Midlands Travel's Travelcards, a product that originated with WMPTE. MCW Metrobus Mark 2 2871 (B871DOM) was one vehicle to be so adorned and was seen on Colmore Row, Birmingham on 8 September 1990, working a Bristol Road service which had by then relinquished its Navigation Street terminus for a circuit of the city centre.

▶ Memories of being able to smoke on buses now only exist with the older generation who saw it reduced initially to the upper deck and the rear of single-deckers then to just the rear of the upper deck before it was prohibited around 1990, at least by West Midlands Travel. Soon after delivery, Alexander RH bodied Scania N113DRB 3201 (H201LOM) was given an all-over-advert representing a countryside scene as an analogue to fresh air. Later versions of clean air advertising would normally refer to reductions of emissions from the vehicles, a future goal when 3201 was seen in Birmingham's Bull Ring on 8 May 1993.

▲ 2975 (E975VUK), numerically the first MCW Metrobus Mark 2A, was another of the first batch of them to gain an all-over-advert whilst based at Perry Barr garage, retaining fleet colours on the front. Mercury Communications, a subsidiary of Cable & Wireless, was an early competitor to BT in the field of communications but the name was dropped in 1997 in favour of its parent. one2one was later sold to Deutsche Telekom and rebranded T-Mobile. Note the 'small print' on the lower body side of 2975 as it took on passengers in Corporation Street, Birmingham on 23 July 1995 for a service 91 journey to the Pheasey estate on the Walsall boundary. The location is a stop on the West Midlands Metro in 2024.

86

◀ Following the arrival of the Scanias at Birmingham Central garage, the early MCW Metrobus Mark 2As moved to Perry Barr garage to work the nominally 'express' routes to the Sutton Coldfield area as shown by 2976 (E976VUK) as it descended Carrs Lane, Birmingham on 4 December 1993. It carried an in-house all-over-advert for WM Holidays, an activity given more prominence following ESOP.

◀ New WMBuses Yardley Wood fleetnames on a silver background have been applied to Leyland Lynx 1093 (G93EOG) which carried advertising for Prophets Garage, the local BMW dealership, for a number of years albeit retaining fleet colours on the front. On 21 April 1995, it was seen in Birmingham's Bull Ring working service 2 from its home garage.

◀ Rear end only advertisements proved popular for businesses wishing to promote themselves to drivers of vehicles who may be following the bus. Coach & Motor Works Ltd of Wolverhampton was one, claiming to be 'The Accident Repair Specialists' on the rear of MCW Metrobus Mark 2 2441 (NOA441X) seen in Dudley bus station in February 1993. It still has the large lower deck rear window initially fitted to the Metrobus Mark 2s but replaced at refurbishment.

87

▶ Bus tickets became a form of lottery ticket in 1994 when West Midlands Travel introduced its 'Match and Win' promotion. A high-profile advert for it appeared on MCW Metrobus Mark 2 2576 (POG576Y) which was seen in the traffic queue along Birmingham's Smallbrook Queensway on a very wet 4 June.

▲ The Swedish furniture conglomerate IKEA opened its first store in the West Midlands in 1991 at Park Lane in Wednesbury. It quickly developed into a location for a family day out and was promoted as such on MCW Metrobus Mark 2A 3072 (F72XOF), although in common with the majority of all-over-adverts from the WMBuses era, it retained fleet colours on the front. On 7 June 1996, it was seen departing West Bromwich bus station with a 451 service to Sutton Coldfield. National Express West Midlands run a similar service in 2024 which has reverted to number 5, its origin with West Bromwich Corporation.

PART 7
Metrowest and Black Country Buses

The Metrowest business was established by a former WMPTE Dudley driver in 1988 eventually becoming a partnership operating a fleet of 25 vehicles, mainly Leyland Nationals, from premises in Coseley. On 14 July 1993, West Midlands Travel obtained a controlling interest, full control being realised on 30 September 1993 when the operation was transferred to a wholly owned West Midlands Travel subsidiary, Black Country Buses. It quickly grew to operate a complimentary network to its parent, including supporting the redistribution of services after Dudley garage was required to close in 1993 to make way for the town's bypass. A similar redistribution took place later in the year as HartsHill garage closed, eliminating the properties acquired from Midland Red in 1973.

After West Midlands Travel sold its whole production batch of 50 Alexander bodied Volvo Ailsas to London Transport in 1987, they were moved on after around three years of service. Three examples would return to the West Midlands joining operators in competition with their former owners. On West Midlands Travel's acquisition of Tame Valley, the pair of Ailsas nominally regained their old numbers but were not used and sold on almost immediately. The third one, 4746 (JOV746P) had joined the Metrowest fleet in 1992 and was seen on 5 May 1993 in Dudley bus station, sporting a very smart repaint and its old number. It would not be used after West Midlands Travel's majority shareholding acquisition and was sold at the end of July to West Yorkshire's Ailsa specialist operator, Black Prince.

▲ A second operation was registered by Metrowest's proprietors in 1992 with the title Challenger, applying a brown and cream livery to some Leyland Nationals including HHA122L seen freshly painted in Dudley bus station during October 1992. The bus had originally entered service with Midland Red at Worcester and would later revert to green as 1722 in the Black Country Buses fleet. On the demise of the latter, it would be stored before moving to the North East Bus operation when approaching 25 years old.

▶ Following the acquisition by West Midlands Travel, there was an influx of Leyland Nationals from the parent fleet to cater for increased activity. Some of them entered service with Black Country Buses in a grey primer with Metrowest fleetnames added. 1468 (ROK468M) was one of these as seen on 16 October 1993 in Dudley bus station alongside vehicles of competitors Stevensons and The Birmingham Coach Company (The forerunner of what is Diamond Bus in 2024).

◀ Six 10.3m Leyland Nationals were acquired by Metrowest from London Buses in 1991 and these were numbered consecutively from 1901 on transfer to Black Country Buses. On 31 August 1993, 1904 (THX267S) was seen leaving Dudley bus station for Wolverhampton on the D25 service that competed with the West Midlands Travel 125 service established back in Midland Red days.

▶ Black Country Buses later received dual-purpose seated Leyland National 1854 (TVP854S) which was distinguished by receiving a cream roof on repaint. Another grey Leyland National, 1485 (TOE485N), stood behind it in Dudley bus station on 16 October 1993.

▶ MCW Metroriders were also transferred to Black Country Buses, usually in the green colour scheme but, following a previous hire spell with GM Buses, 667 (F667YOG) was in a brown scheme not unlike the Challenger colours, albeit with Metrowest fleetnames. In 1993/4, it was usual to see a Black Country Buses Metrorider parked at this point in Dudley bus station as a crew vehicle, 667 had been allocated the duty on 29 November 1993.

▶ Towards the end of Black Country Buses existence as a subsidiary, some of West Midlands Travel's Leyland National 2s were transferred in, repainted in Metrowest green and cream with the strapline of 'The Black Country's Green Buses' added. Seen in Dudley bus station on 11 April 1994, 1045 (DOC45V) was one of these. It would later go on hire to British Bus in north-west England before moving to National Express' associate operation, Highland Country in Fort William.

PART 8
Smiths of Shennington (Your Bus)

◀ Smiths of Shennington adopted a GMPTE style livery for its Your Bus operation, influenced no doubt by the acquisition of double-deckers from that source initially. A later recruit from the same source but arriving via intermediate owners was Leyland National 100 (JNA587N), the only one of its type left in the fleet when the business was acquired by West Midlands Travel. The colourful Your Bus fleetname is prominent as it descended Bradford Street in Birmingham on 15 June 1994. Most of the background buildings have subsequently been swept away for redevelopment.

▶ The Your Bus operation commenced with second-hand double-deckers but these were very much in the minority by 1993. The final acquisitions as an independent company were several Leyland Atlantean AN68/1Rs from South Yorkshire Travel including dual-doorway Alexander AL bodied 62 (CWG698V) seen departing Birmingham on 16 August 1993 with a late evening peak journey on service 53Y that would extend to the Your Bus garage in Alcester. At the height of Your Bus operations, Alcester residents had a cheap and frequent commuter service to Birmingham as most vehicle positioning journeys were registered services. This facility was lost when the Your Bus operation moved to Miller Street in Birmingham. Double-deck operation nominally ceased on the acquisition by West Midlands Travel although a pair of Atlanteans are reported to have been re-activated for a very short time to cover former Stevensons services.

93

▶ Several MCW Metroriders were transferred to Your Bus for the Burton-on-Trent operation including 161 (D613NOE) seen at the junction of High Street and New Street in the town on 8 July 1994. With the background buildings little changed, this location remains the hub of the town's bus network in 2024.

▼ West Midlands Travel used its recently acquired Your Bus subsidiary to mount a competitive challenge to Stevensons on its home territory in Burton-on-Trent in 1994. Full size vehicle requirements were met from the fleet of Ikarus bodied DAF SB220s built up by Your Bus, supported by Leyland Nationals from the reserve fleet. One of the former, 19 (J37GCX), emphasised the level of competition in the town as it led a Derby BlueBus and two Stevensons vehicles out of New Street on 8 July 1884. It had been equipped with appropriate destination blinds for the assignment.

The rebranding introduced from late 1994 also encompassed the Your Bus subsidiary as WM YOURBUS. The fleetnames are seen here applied to Leyland National 113 (PUK633R), one of the large number of the type acquired from Midland Red West in 1994, most of which would be stored and sold on without entering service. On 27 April 1996, it was departing from Birmingham's Bull Ring on a 54 service to the city's south-western suburbs.

▲ WM YOURBUS had a limited requirement for double-deck vehicles which was later met with the transfer of vehicles from the core fleet, retaining their original colour scheme with new fleetnames and numbers. MCW bodied Leyland Fleetline FE30 6979 (WDA679T), with its new number 142 not shown, was one of the vehicles involved and was seen in the operations base in Miller Street on 13 July 1996.

▶ Your Bus invested in two batches of underfloor engine single-deckers with Plaxton Derwent bodywork, eight Leyland Tigers and eleven Volvo B10Ms. One of the latter, 155 (H155SKU) was seen on 24 June 1996 passing the junction of Heath Mill Lane and High Street Deritend in Birmingham. All the buildings in the background remain extant in 2024 as part of the Zellig complex, the bank is a café-bar and the former Birds premises behind trades as the Custard Factory. West Midlands Metro tracks occupy much of the foreground roadspace.